CAROLYN T. LINN

HEAVEN IS AMAZING

A COMPELLING MESSAGE OF HOPE AND ENCOURAGEMENT

READERSMAGNET, LLC

READER REVIEWS

I think your book is great. Thanks for letting me read it…..I didn't want to wait any longer to reply. Well done!

T.N.

I just wanted to thank you once again for providing me with the vivid and beautiful picture of heaven. Although we still struggle with the indescribable loss, it is comforting at those quiet and peaceful moments during the day to know how whole, perfect, and happy [our grandson] is.

D.F.

I have never before read such a "realistic" description of heaven. I am not acquainted with the books and articles that you cite in your bibliography, but assume they are reports from "near death" experiences, and the source for some of your graphic descriptions of things that await us in heaven.

I especially latched onto the idea that family members observe when one of us is passing into eternity, then hasten to welcome us. We lost an infant son…..I have sometimes thought that he will be the first one to welcome us and show us around heaven!

Your writing is clear and engaging - - easy to read, easy to follow. My guess is that you'll be hearing from some readers who have lost loved ones, asking whether you can give them a few more details!

L.C.

I have never before read such "realistic" descriptions of heaven. I contacted the author and found she has been researching her topic for many years, both through study of Scripture and reports from people who have "near death" experiences. The writing is clear and engaging - - easy to read, easy to follow. For some the topic might come across as speculation or imagination, but for those who have recently lost loved ones, it could well be a word of comfort.

L.C.

My Bible Study group covered 'Heaven is Amazing' in four weeks. We typically share each book by reading aloud and pausing to discuss whenever there is a question or comment. I'd say everyone found your words interesting and helpful. Rev. B---- said "I loved the imaginative infant nursery where angels cared for the babies. Heaven is a creative fun place where we will be safe".

Dr. D---- thought your book was inspirational and thought provoking. I agree. Your strong faith was evident throughout the book and served to augment the scriptures you frequently quoted.

Overall, I feel many of my personal stumbling blocks about heaven were removed. By your inclusion and unscrambling of several scriptures within the text, the reader gains a clearer perspective of what Heaven may be like. I now see Heaven as a boundless spiritual oasis. Unfortunately, our earthly perception of Heaven is often limited by a lack of imagination and/or a spiritual shortfall in understanding just how powerful God can be.

Thanks again for alerting me of your book. It was an educational treat and a wonderful opportunity for me to see your deep faith in action.

R.W.

I liked it all. …She had alot of wonderful thoughts and Heaven to look forward to. Very well written also.

B.S.

I found it to be interesting reading from an interesting perspective. The author's conviction to her faith is admirable and inspiring.

G.K.

DEDICATION

Soli Deo Gloria!
(Glory to God Alone!)

ACKNOWLEDGMENTS

THE SUBJECT OF HEAVEN has fascinated me since my husband died suddenly about ten years ago. I have often wondered what he is doing in the presence of Jesus and the heavenly Father whom he studied as an academician and tried to follow as a faithful disciple.

My husband grew up in a family that valued the Word of God. Conversations discussing the fine points of Scripture were common in his household. My pastor father also led discussions about Christian life and the hereafter as a dedicated servant of God.

During my years of widowhood I have witnessed an increase in the recorded incidents of people being taken to heaven or hell and back. Through near-death experiences or supernatural visions these visitors have told amazing details of what they have seen. Each time I hear a new story I add another thread to the tapestry of heaven being woven in my mind. The picture is developing into a scene of incredible splendor and indescribable love created by our amazing God. It is time for me to share the compilation of insights I have accumulated thus far.

For reading my manuscript and giving me suggestions and resources, I would like to thank my sister, the Rev. Dr. Arlynne C. Turnquist. I was also encouraged to continue this project by my pastor, the Rev. Ted Niemi. Bishop John David Schofield was excited enough to offer his insights, corrections and theological advice. And university professor Dr. Mary Pranzo, my wise friend who cautioned me about the pitfalls of publishing, saw merit in the end product and agreed it was time to share these revelations with others.

My publishers, with their Christian mission, provided the guidance and expertise to make this book an attractive package that would be a vehicle for ministering the message of salvation to a hungry world.

To all of these worthy friends, I say thank you. May our wonderful Lord Jesus Christ and His Father in heaven receive the glory!

CONTENTS

1   Why Write About Heaven? 11

2   Death: Transition To Heaven 17

3   Heavenly Life 23

4   Heavenly Beings 31

5   Heavenly Places 41

6   Heavenly Entertainment 53

7   Heavenly Love: "Song Of Songs" 59

8   Heavenly Worship 73

9   Hell: Don't Go There! 77

Endnotes 85

Bibliography 87

About The Author 89

CHAPTER 1

WHY WRITE ABOUT HEAVEN?

Life passes at an incredible speed. At various times we labor through harsh days and seemingly endless nights. At other times joyful moments fly by with a sweetness that allows us to savor them forever. Our heads may be full of gray hair, but it seems that only yesterday we were romping through the innocence of childhood. Now our aging bodies betray the years that have consumed us.

This writer has lived a lot of life, but these last few years have been among the happiest I have known. One of the reasons is that I've been blessed to have wonderful opportunities to travel the world. Each time I take a trip I enhance the experience by preparing ahead, learning all I can about the destination.

Such research gives me a sense of anticipation which means I can savor the delights of where I'm going. I learn about the history, beauty, highlights and people. I also enjoy knowing the spiritual background of a place; perhaps it is or has been a center of faith for its citizens. Symbols of worship may be evidence that God has been important in the history of a community. Great cathedrals or famous patrons of faith may be among the location's greatest attractions.

Because of my pre-reading I can make a two-week trip an experience that lasts many months. Plus when I return I have invariably picked up books along the way. As I read these books and match information with my photographs I am able to complete my understanding of places and people. What began merely as a tour destination now becomes part of my life; I make it "my own."

In these faraway places I also buy gifts for people who are dear to me, especially family members: siblings, young people like my grandchildren, great nieces and nephews. Perhaps someday they will be interested in visiting famous sites because of my exposure to them. It is part of their education, just as it is part of mine.

I explain this process and relate it to my travels because at this stage in life I am thinking ahead and preparing for when I will someday take the "ultimate trip" at the end of my life. Since I believe in Jesus Christ as the one who loves me and has died for my sins I expect to go to heaven.

I lost my husband to death nearly a decade ago, and I have been curious about heaven since then. I trust he is there, and I wonder what he is doing. My interest has led me to many books written by people who have had enlightenment about heaven or have had near-death experiences and have reported what they saw.

In fact, my own pastor father on his death bed, As told by my oldest sister who was present, had a vision of what awaited him in heaven. He was in awe! His comment was, "It would take a lifetime to describe what I saw."

Similarly, my maternal grandfather had a glimpse of glory as he died. He explained his epiphany by saying, "I see Jesus." Ironically, his death occurred on January 6, the church festival of Epiphany.

Likewise my husband, shortly before his death following surgery, said he had seen Jesus. I have often heard testimony of that declaration from clergy and health care workers who have been in the presence of dying people. I believe they do see Jesus. One of my husband's favorite Bible verses was a promise of the heavenly kingdom where Christ shall reign for eternity with God the Father.

> *"The kingdoms of this world have become the kingdoms of our Lord and of His Christ, and He shall reign forever and ever!" (Revelation 11:15).*

I believe the God of heaven has given a vision of life after death to many people these days. As I have read these accounts I have felt joy and excitement. Now I want to write down the information so I can relish the destination in the same way I do my earthly travels.

My life has included many challenges, living forty-one years with a wonderful, brilliant, God-fearing man who shortly into our marriage was diagnosed with schizophrenia, paranoid-type. After being stabilized on medication following numerous traumatic episodes, he was able to have a productive career, teaching part-time at the university level. Raising a family with illness in the home, however, left deep scars on our two children and me. Only the Lord in His mercy and love is bringing hope and joy out of our brokenness.

Because I have passed the biblically allotted years of three score and ten, I expect my final journey could take place anytime. This year is the fiftieth anniversary of our marriage, an event I celebrate even in my widowhood, because of God's goodness. I believe marriage is forever, and I look forward to being reunited in heaven with my husband who is now whole and perfect.

By writing down my preparation for the journey to heaven, I can also share with others what I learn as a way to encourage them on their pathway through life, especially as they near death.

During the last few years I have assimilated into my mind material from a number of sources, read and spoken. This information has crystallized as categories in my thinking, which I present here.

Many of the detailed descriptions come directly from author Kat Kerr and her books *Revealing Heaven* (Xulon Press, 2007) and *Revealing Heaven II* (Xulon Press, 2010). These books are available at <u>www.revealingheaven.com</u> or <u>www.xulonpress.com</u>.

I have gleaned insight from the numerous "trips" she has taken to heaven, even though I cannot explain how she has gone there. Her accounts describe vividly the sights she has seen; and I do believe God has been her revelator. Other bits of heaven I have gathered from accounts of those who have had brief visits to God's eternal home before being brought back to earth to complete the life God had planned for them.

Believers, I am sure, begin their heavenly experience while still on earth as God answers their request for Him to enter their lives. At that time the Holy Spirit comes to dwell within God's child and begins the work of change from the inside out.

> *"And we all, with unveiled face, beholding the glory of the Lord, are being changed into his likeness from one degree of glory to another; for this comes from the Lord who is the Spirit." (2 Corinthians 3:18 RSV)*

The journey to heaven is merely the next phase of this relationship with a God who loves us beyond imagination.

A couple of phrases come to mind when I think of approaching heaven. One is to live in the "eternity of the moment," which says to me that life now is part of heaven as we share God's kingdom with others, bringing them with us into eternity. Another phrase I like describes the joy of heaven: "All the things that make life happy: this is heaven!"

In the pages ahead I will attempt to organize material from the sources above, describing what happens at the moment of death and what we will encounter in our heavenly home.

Since God is far greater than we can imagine, however, the descriptions here are only a glimpse of the future. Each child of God will have a different experience uniquely designed by our loving God. I have included Bible verses that support the information throughout the text.

The material is divided into sections as follows:

Death: Transition to Heaven—What happens when we die? Are we transported directly to heaven? Who is there? What do we see?

Heavenly Life—What kind of environment can we expect? Will our life resemble what we know on earth?

Heavenly Beings—What kind of beings will we be? What other creatures has God placed in the heavenly kingdom? What about babies and children? Are pets in heaven?

Heavenly Places—How will we spend time during our eternity in heaven? Can we visit with friends? Can we get married? Do we have sex in heaven? Can we learn new things? Are there opportunities to use our talents?

Heavenly Entertainment—Is heaven a fun place, or is it dull and boring? How does God prove He wants us to be happy?

Heavenly Love: "Song of Songs"—What is the reason God has prepared heaven for His people? How can we understand God's love? What does God desire from His people in eternal life?

Heavenly Worship—How do we worship God and show our love for Him? Are there cultural activities with music, art, dance or drama?

Hell: Don't Go There!—What happens if heaven is not our destiny? What happens if we go to hell? Will we ever have a second chance at heaven?

CHAPTER 2

DEATH: TRANSITION TO HEAVEN

THE PICTURE AT DEATH seems to be universal from many sources. It is described as glorious. We take our last breath, and our spirits leave our bodies. We float upward weightlessly, free of any sickness or affliction that brought us to this point. We are aware of people around us as we die, but we are unable to communicate with them. We may see a bright light as if rays from the sun fill the space. Colors emanate from the rays overtaking us in splendor. As we rise out of our bodies, we feel no pain or fear. We are overwhelmed by a sweetness coming from God's love.

As we leave our earthly bodies we become young and vital-looking again without any effects of age or disease.

I've heard our permanent life-age in heaven is about the same as Jesus when He died at thirty-three. The eternal life of God flows through us, and we feel wonderful; we still have our senses. In fact, they are enhanced. We can see, feel, hear, touch and taste with greater acuity, but we have left our bodies and have become spirit beings.

After His resurrection Jesus came to His disciples as a spirit body that was recognizable to other people. Jesus described Himself this way:

> *"Behold My hands and My feet, that it is I Myself. Handle Me and see, for a spirit does not have flesh and bones as you see I have…He showed them His hands and His feet" (Luke 24:39—40).*

Jesus Himself or angels will appear and escort us to heaven, calling us by name. Around us will be overwhelming light, peace and joy. We know we are in a safe place. Scripture verifies the immediacy of our destination.

> *"And Jesus said to [the thief on the cross next to him], 'Assuredly, I say to you, today you will be with Me in paradise'" (Luke 23:43).*
>
> *"For we walk by faith, not by sight. We are confident, yes, well pleased rather to be absent from the body and to be present with the Lord" (2 Corinthians 5:7—8).*

Various vehicles will be used to carry us to heaven. One is a "transport"[1] which is a heavenly cable-car-like structure that allows us to see the universe passing by as we ascend to the third heaven where God dwells. In the New Testament Paul talks of a man being transported to heaven.

"I know a man in Christ—such a one was caught up to the third heaven…whether in the body or out of the body I do not know, God knows—" (2 Corinthians 12:2—3).

These transports are piloted by angels or by special beings with the ability to welcome people graciously to the heavenly kingdom. When the transport stops we are escorted by other angels or people who take us along an exceptionally beautiful path. Everything in heaven is alive; flowers and trees have life to them. One has the feeling that all is right in this place, drawing us into a peace that passes all understanding. Family and friends who have gone before us rush to welcome us joyfully, celebrating our arrival. We see generation after generation of people who have been influential in our knowledge of God and our growth in faith. They all look wonderful!

We advance toward the heavenly gates, our hearts exploding with the love of God. Heaven is the most brilliant, glorious place imaginable, causing all other beauty to pale in comparison and fade from our memories. We pass through the heavenly gates and are taken to the home that has been lovingly prepared for us. Our Lord has created an environment that is uniquely designed for each person. Friends and family have filled it with gifts to prepare for our arrival. We have the sensation of being home where we belong.

"In My Father's house are many mansions…I go to prepare a place for you…I will come again and receive you to Myself; that where I am, there you may be also" (John 14:2—3).

The architecture, interior design and landscaping of our heavenly home have been chosen carefully to please us. Even our pets, recreated by our loving Father, will be waiting for us. Now is the time to greet and rejoice with friends and family. We are overwhelmed by the powerful love of God and the beauty all around as we experience the sights, sounds and aromas of heaven.

If we haven't already seen Him, Jesus comes. He is dressed in a white robe, whiter than any white we have seen before. His eyes are sparkling and beautiful beyond description. He looks at us lovingly and calls us by name. Jesus escorts us into the throne room where the redeemed and the angels worship and rejoice together, singing, dancing and bowing before the throne.

> *"Immediately I was in the Spirit; and behold, a throne set in heaven and One sat on the throne. And He who sat there was like a jasper and a sardius stone in appearance; and there was a rainbow around the throne, in appearance like an emerald" (Revelation 4:2—3).*

Jesus communicates with us thought-to-thought without saying a word. He joins His people as they dance together, adoring the Father who is seated in brilliance on the throne. Other people will raise banners and dance before God to demonstrate their passion for Jesus and the Father. As the dancers run, the images on their banners come alive and join in praise to the Holy Trinity. The glory becomes so rich and heavy that all in the room fall on their faces, soaking in the love that comes in waves from the Father's heart.

The throne in the center of the room is high and lifted up, enabling all people to be near the Father and Jesus, who sits at God's right hand. Steps lead up to the throne; the redeemed are welcome whenever they wish to visit with the Father or Jesus. Praise in the room is electric!

> *"And in the midst of the throne, and around the throne, were four living creatures full of eyes in front and in back…And they do not rest day or night, saying: 'Holy, holy, holy, Lord God Almighty, who was and is and is to come!'" (Revelation 4:6,8).*

A rainbow encircles the throne in radiant shades and tints of color far more glorious than what we see on earth. Colors virtually explode in God's presence. Our eyes are full of wonder, beholding the glory of the Father as He declares His love for us. Fire and lightning proceed from His presence, and awe falls over the throne room; everyone turns to watch as we are welcomed. We have never felt so alive and so totally comfortable, knowing we are truly Home.

God draws us to Himself and holds us. We feel the joy of total love and acceptance engulfing us. In Him we are made truly whole!

After a time of communion with the Godhead we are taken on an extensive tour of heaven by our family or friends. What we see is unbelievable!

> *"Eye has not seen, nor ear heard, nor have entered into the heart of man the things which God has prepared for those who love him" (1 Corinthians 2:9).*

Our arrival in heaven is complete; we have entered eternal life where we have a new home; we have seen Jesus and been in the presence of God the Father. Our joy overflows as we renew friendships with those already in heaven. We don't even remember what we have left behind on earth. Those memories fade away. We now live in a place of ultimate love, joy and peace. Soon we will begin to experience heavenly life.

CHAPTER 3

HEAVENLY LIFE

God with His People

IN HIS HEAVENLY KINGDOM God is ever with His people, loving them, teaching them, showing them His mysteries. God and His people delight in each other.

> *"Behold, the tabernacle of God is with men, and He will dwell with them, and they shall be His people. God Himself will be with them and be their God" (Revelation 21:3).*

There is no more sorrow in heaven, only laughter and joy, coming down from the author of life and the giver of all good things.

> *"God will wipe away every tear from their eyes; there shall be no more death, nor sorrow, nor crying. There shall be no more pain, for the former things have passed away" (Revelation 21:4).*

God fills heaven with His glory; there is no night, only continual day, in the presence of Almighty God. Light is a vehicle of creation God uses to supply the needs of His people.

> *"I saw no temple in it, for the Lord God Almighty and the Lamb are its temple." (Revelation 21:22—23).*

> *"There shall be no night there: They need no lamp nor light of the sun for the Lord God gives them light" (Revelation 22:5).*

Water and food are given freely in heaven, not that they are needed for sustenance because spirit beings do not need nutrition; but the joy of nourishment contributes to the fullness of life available through the heavenly Father. Water is crystal clear and always as near as the throne of God. A crystal sea forms in God's presence, and it flows throughout the heavenly kingdom.

> *"Before the throne there was a sea of glass, like crystal" (Revelation 4:6a).*

> *"And he showed me a pure river of water of life, clear as crystal, proceeding from the throne of God and of the Lamb" (Revelation 22:1).*

Bodies consume food, but it is for pleasure, not nourishment. Jesus' resurrection body was the first example of a spirit body, and He assured the disciples He could take in food.

> *"[Jesus] said to [His disciples], 'Have you any food here?' So they gave Him a piece of broiled fish and some honey-comb. And He took it and ate in their presence" (Luke 24:41—43).*

Golden Streets

Streets in heaven have a transparency that reflects the glory of God, creating a golden glow. You can see the image of your spirit being when you look down at yourself in the streets.

> *"The street of the city was pure gold, like transparent glass" (Revelation 21:21b).*

Streets crisscross heaven, leading to mansions, shops and the wonderful places God has created for His people. Vehicles of all types—chariots, motorcycles, antique cars, trolleys, futuristic models—also traverse the golden streets.[2] Sometimes the streets themselves move, similar to moving walkways in airports on earth.

The only fuel used in heaven, besides the movement of the wind, is light. Roads of pure light transport people from place to place above the ground. Light is a creative force and the product used to create material objects.[3] God's power embodies all things.

> *"The city had no need of the sun or of the moon to shine in it, for the glory of God illuminated it. The Lamb is its light" (Revelation 21:23).*

Life is way ahead of the best practices on earth. Heaven is, indeed, a supernatural place!

Gemstones

Gemstones represent the love of the Father's heart, the reward for those who suffer on earth; they shine with the light of God's presence.

> *"O you afflicted one, tossed with tempest, and not comforted. Behold, I will lay your stones with colorful gems, and lay your foundations with sapphires. I will make your pinnacles of rubies, your gates of crystal, and all your walls of precious stones" (Isaiah 54:11—12).*

The sparkling beauty of gemstones glistens everywhere in heaven, even in the walls of the city and in its gates.

> *"The construction of [the city's] wall was of jasper; and the city was pure gold, like clear glass. The foundations of the wall of the city were adorned with all kinds of precious stones: jasper...sapphire...chalcedony... emerald...sardonyx...sardius...chrysolite...beryl... topaz...chrysoprase...jacinth...amethyst. The twelve gates were twelve pearls; each individual gate was of one pearl" (Revelation 21:18—21a).*

Food

Food is consumed because it is a pleasure to eat, but eating doesn't produce problems in the body from abuse or overuse the way it does on earth. Food is not taken from killed animals, fish or fowl. It is produced by light, but it tastes and smells more delicious than food on earth. We can still eat whatever we like; we just need to state our order, and it will appear. Pleasant foods will be available just for the plucking whenever we desire them.

> *"In the middle of its street, and on either side of the river, was the tree of life, which bore twelve fruits, each tree yielding its fruit every month. The leaves of the tree were for the healing of the nations" (Revelation 22:2).*

People on earth who had talents in food preparation will open restaurants when they are in heaven, so the eternal population will have places to continue to enjoy all the pleasantness of consuming foods.

Clothes

People in heaven have spiritual bodies that don't require the care of earthly bodies, but spirit beings wear clothes. They wear gowns and robes. The gowns are brilliant white, but the robes are designed and embellished according to one's level of reward and service to the Lord. Some robes are so gloriously decorated that they are, indeed, works of art. The exceptional garments do not engender envy or jealousy; rather, God's glory is reflected through their beauty and everyone rejoices in His goodness. Each spirit being declares God's great mercy through what he or she wears.

Spirit beings wear different outfits for different occasions, the way we do on earth. Their clothes have significance, not as a source of human pride, but as evidence of the glory of God that has been manifest in them. A tunic outfit is a normal part of everyone's wardrobe and is visible all over heaven in every imaginable style, color and fabric. Some people with a talent for tailoring use their skills to develop new fabrics and garments.

Crowns will be part of each person's heavenly adornment, too, a reward for suffering. The beauty of the crown indicates the intensity of the struggle on earth. Others will recognize the victory of overcomers by the crowns they wear.

> *"Blessed is the man who endures temptation; for when he has been approved, he will receive the crown of life which the Lord has promised to those who love Him" (James 1:12).*

> *"Do not fear any of those things which you are about to suffer…Be faithful until death, and I will give you the crown of life" (Revelation 2:10).*

Shopping

As it is for some on earth, shopping is an enjoyable pastime in heaven but without the need to buy and sell. Everything is free. People will "buy" what pleases them or find gifts for loved ones to place in the mansions being readied for them.

Treasure in heaven is measured differently from on earth. Material goods have no value in the heavenly life. The only treasure we take with us to heaven is people who know God and good deeds that are accomplished to the glory of the Father.

> *"Do not lay up for yourselves treasures on earth, where moth and rust destroy and where thieves break in and steal; but lay up for yourselves treasures in heaven, where neither moth nor rust destroys and where thieves do not break in and steal. For where your treasure is, there your heart will be also" (Matthew 6:19).*

Everyone living in heaven shares their gifts and talents with everyone else. Those who created merchandise on earth will continue to use their talent in heaven. Those who are gifted with providing services will continue their good work in the next life. For these goods and services there is no cost to anyone; money doesn't exist.[4] There are shops in which to find precious materials, items of pleasure, jewelry, perfumes, oils and fabrics so dazzling they could only be produced in God's heavenly kingdom.

> *"Seek first the kingdom of God and His righteousness, and all these things [that you need] will be added to you"* (Matthew 6:33).

The greatest inheritance anyone can leave children and grandchildren is faith in Jesus Christ. These family members then have the opportunity to receive salvation for themselves and entrance into God's heavenly kingdom.

Heavenly life is beyond anything we can imagine, far beyond any earthly comforts or joys in today's world. Existence in heaven for us is as advanced as life in our century would be for peasants in the Middle Ages or for citizens in Jesus' day.

These glimpses of heavenly life are only hints of what awaits God's people. God has far more abundance than our hearts can hold. Once heavenly life becomes familiar, we will find an array of heavenly heavenly helpers all around us with angels and created beings doing everyday tasks.

CHAPTER 4

HEAVENLY BEINGS

Angels

ANGELS COME IN MANY varieties and sizes. They can be as
small as humans or as tall as a twenty-storey building. They
are defenders and protectors. Warrior angels are strong and
muscular, ready to do battle. Guardian angels are assigned
to each person at birth. Children are especially precious to
the Lord, and their angels have God's full attention.

> *"Take heed that you do not despise one of these little ones,*
> *for I say to you that in heaven their angels always see the*
> *face of My father who is in heaven" (Matthew 18:10).*

On earth angels protect and guard people from harm
and report to heaven concerning their spiritual growth.
Angelic beings can and do change their appearance. They
reside quietly and anonymously in the spiritual realm of

earth. They have emotions and are elated when people make progress in living and acting according to God's will. The purpose of angels is to do the bidding of the Father, to please Him at all times. He assigns them tasks to care for people. Angels use every power available in heaven to fulfill their assignments. They are diligent and responsible.

> *"For He shall give His angels charge over you, to keep you in all your ways. In their hands they shall bear you up, lest you dash your foot against a stone"* (Psalm 91:11—12).

> *"The angel of the Lord encamps all around those who fear Him, and delivers them"* (Psalm 34:7).

Angels give visions of the future to the prophets, according to God's plan of revelation.

> *"Michael, one of the chief princes, came to help me… Now I have come to make you understand what will happen to your people in the latter days, for the vision refers to many days yet to come"* (Daniel 10:13—14).

David Wilkerson, the late evangelist who ministered to the drug culture of New York City in the 1960s, describes the work of angels when Jacob saw them on a ladder to heaven.

"God was drawing back the curtain and showing… [what] was going on all the time. All those angels were on assignment—going back and forth to the earth to guide and lead God's people, minister to them, camp around them, warn them, protect them, guard them, provide for their needs…That ladder is still there! And those same angels have not aged a single hour since Jacob saw them.

In fact, they are still working and ministering on our behalf today."[5]

Living Creatures

God created a species called living creatures. They are not animals, walking on all four legs, but they stand upright and are intelligent beings. They have garments of transparent, glistening material, through which hundreds of eyes are looking all around them. They also have six wings with eyes in all the feathers. Four of these living creatures stand at the corners of the throne of God and continually proclaim the holiness of God. One creature has the head of a lion, a second the head of an ox, a third the head of an eagle and the last the head of a man.

"The four living creatures and the twenty-four elders fell down before the Lamb, each having a harp, and golden bowls full of incense, which are the prayers of the saints" (Revelation 5:8).

Seraphim

The seraphim are another category of heavenly beings that fly back and forth over the Father as He sits on His throne. On earth they hover over those who minister to the Lord, blessing them with God's glory.

"Above [the throne] stood seraphim; each one had six wings; with two he covered his face, with two he covered his feet, and with two he flew. And one cried to another and said: Holy, holy, holy is the Lord of hosts; the whole earth is full of His glory!" (Isaiah 6:2—3).

Cherubim

Another type of angelic beings is called cherubim, who hovered over the Ark of the Covenant in the Old Testament tabernacle in the wilderness.

> *"Above [the Ark of the Covenant] were the cherubim of glory overshadowing the mercy seat" (Hebrews 9:5).*

They also were seen in Ezekiel's vision of the throne of God and were part of the glory of God. Cherubim, like seraphim, are full of eyes.

> *"Each [cherubim] had four faces and each one four wings, and the likeness of the hands of a man was under their wings" (Ezekiel 10:21).*

A nameless form of created beings in heaven is similar to humans except they are transparent. They are friendly and know people by name, acting as hosts and hostesses at some of the locations for entertainment and education in heaven.[6]

Spirit Beings

From the beginning of time God's spirit existed and moved silently over creation.

> *"In the beginning God created the heavens and the earth. The earth was without form and void, and darkness was upon the face of the deep; and the Spirit of God was moving over the face of the waters." (Genesis 1:1—2 RSV)*

Beginning with Adam and Eve, God breathed a life-giving spirit into human beings. Every person born has been given the breath of life that comes from our heavenly Father. In Him exist life, love and creation; inside the Father of Lights are not fleshly organs; inside Him eternity dwells.[7]

When Job questioned God's authority, claiming his innocence of sufficient guilt to have brought about the tragedies in his life, his false friends mocked Job's defense by comparing Job to the mighty God, a God from whom spirits come.

> *"To whom have you uttered words? And whose spirit came from you?" (Job 26:4).*

The writer of the book of Hebrews, in chapter 12, verse 9, calls God the "Father of spirits." Indeed, life from God is what was breathed into the human form of Adam to give him existence.

> *"And the Lord God formed man of the dust of the ground, and breathed into his nostrils the breath of life; and man became a living being." (Genesis 2:7)*

The reverse is true at the time of death:

> *"When the dust will return to the earth as it was, and the spirit will return to God who gave it" (Ecclesiastes 12:7).*

When in His divine wisdom God calls us to become human beings, God initiates a very special process. He breathes life into what is conceived in human flesh, and that pulsating tissue mass becomes a living being. Luke writes in Acts that God considers people His offspring, the product of His divine mind and creation.

> *"Therefore since we are the offspring of God, we ought not to think that the Divine Nature is like gold or silver or stone, something shaped by art and man's devising"* (Acts 17:29).

The psalmist declares God's knowledge of human development in the womb before birth.

> *"For you formed my inward parts; you covered me in my mother's womb. I will praise You, for I am fearfully and wonderfully made; marvelous are Your works"* (Psalm 139:13—14).

> *"My frame was not hidden from You, when I was made in secret, and skillfully wrought in the lowest part of the earth. Your eyes saw my substance, being yet unformed"* (Psalm 139: 15—16a).

The prophet Jeremiah reiterates this truth as God says:

> *"Before I formed you in the womb, I knew you; before you were born I sanctified you"* (Jeremiah 1:5).

Not only did God know humans before birth, but all the days of their lives were determined, from the beginning of time.

> *"And in your book they all were written, the days fashioned for me, when as yet there were none of them"* (Psalm 139:16b).

Human life cannot exist without the power of God enabling each breath.

> *"The Spirit of God has made me, and the breath of the Almighty gives me life" (Job 33:4).*

Only the creator God does healing within the body after illness or injury. The medical world can assist, but no human force alone can cause cells to grow and new life to develop.

> *"In Him we live and move and have our being" (Acts 17:28).*

When the human body has passed away in death and becomes a spirit being, it still depends on God for all things, but the human free will has been enveloped into the Father's perfect will.

Like Jesus after His resurrection, spirit beings are spiritual bodies in heaven fully aware of their senses. They see and hear, eat and move, but their bodies don't perform bodily functions, since God provides for all their needs and is their life force. Spiritual beings recognize one another in heaven and have loving relationships with those from earth; but there is no marriage in heaven, and sexual relations are not part of life there.

> *"For when they rise from the dead, they neither marry nor are given in marriage, but are like angels in heaven" (Mark 12:25).*

There is no need to procreate since people are added to heaven by responding on earth to God's invitation to eternal life through Jesus Christ. Sex is for the purpose of multiplying people on earth. Children are a blessing to the human family.

> *"And God blessed them, saying, 'Be fruitful and multiply'" (Genesis 1:22).*
>
> *"Behold, children are a heritage from the Lord, the fruit of the womb is a reward. Like arrows in the hand of the warrior, so are the children of one's youth. Happy is the man who has his quiver full of them." (Psalm 127:3—5)*

The pleasure related to sex increases the incentive of the human race to follow God's directive and people the earth. The intimacy of human love-making enhances the companionship and comfort of the marriage relationship. It is a foretaste of the joy of intimacy with our heavenly Father. In Him is perfect love.

God did not create the earth and then decide to put people on it for the benefit of the earthly planet. He created the earth in order to have a place where a human family could live, reproduce and learn of His love. His desire is that each person develop a relationship with the Father and dwell together in His love for all eternity.

> *"He chose us in Him before the foundation of the world, that we would be holy and blameless before Him in love" (Ephesians 1:4, NASB).*

Babies and Children

Babies and children on earth, delivered to heaven for whatever reason, are lovingly received. Their heavenly Father cherishes each one of them.

Little ones in heaven have a different routine from those on earth. There are no diapers to change and feeding schedules to follow. They do not need sleep the way they do on earth. They do rest, but they also play and learn.

They have God's knowledge and can communicate since they are raised in the perfect love of God. Joy is an automatic part of their lives. Their little faces reflect the glory of God, and they know Him as people will know Him.

"All your children shall be taught by the Lord, and great shall be the peace of your children" (Isaiah 54:13).

Children develop very slowly outside of the timeline of earth, awaiting the parent(s) to come to raise them.[8] Parents who come to heaven enjoy watching each child grow into a happy, complete being.

Children will be raised in a holy, loving atmosphere, waiting for the day when they are joined to their parents or family members with whom they will share eternity. God desires the restoration of families. He allows families to stay connected in heaven, sharing activities and going places together. Spirit beings never forget those who were family members on earth.

The heavenly kingdom includes not only redeemed people but beings that will circulate around the throne of God, doing His bidding and praising His glory. Besides the angels, seraphim, cherubim, living creatures, spirit beings, babies and children described here, only God knows what other heavenly beings will greet those who arrive in heaven. Life in heaven is fully complete with an atmosphere of peace, joy and love. It has beauty for enjoyment, work for accomplishment and activities for participation. Next we examine some of the places God has prepared for His people in heaven.

CHAPTER 5

HEAVENLY PLACES

God has so designed heaven that it is filled with places in which to laugh, learn, grow and receive knowledge of the mysteries of the universe. God has set up restaurants, art galleries, sports arenas, movie theaters, even an amusement park for His people, according to those who have seen glimpses of heaven. There will be places to go, things to do, people to see that will make heavenly life filled with joy and happiness. The destinations described below are just a few of the ways God shows His love for all eternity.

Nurseries[9]

Children have a special place of nurture in heaven. Abortion has cut short the earthly lives of millions of babies before they are born, but not one is lost or discarded by our heavenly Father. Heaven has all of them there.

Little ones are kept in nurseries and cared for by angelic beings that sing to them and rock them in their arms. Jesus receives them and heals the wounds of their hearts and teaches them forgiveness. The breath of God nourishes them as they grow. The nurseries are beautifully bathed in a warm glow. Flowers are everywhere within the space and even growing out of walls. Tiny birds perch on tree branches to sing to the babies. The babies' beds are niches in the wall, with every baby's name etched in the space above. Even unborn babies can have names; each is given a celebration ceremony to secure the child's identity forever.

For daily activity God has created a play pond for little babies to enjoy themselves. Since there is no evil, the babies are allowed to explore the play pond with no adult watching over them. This play pond is filled with the light of God which provides many exciting, creative activities for wee ones. They slide down rainbows; deer come and give rides, as do kangaroos. The little people mount turtle shells to splash in the water or swim with goldfish beneath the surface.

When the children must return to their nurseries, dragonflies are sent to deliver the message. Then little animals carry the babies back to the nurseries where Jesus is waiting to have a party for them. No child is ever without care and love. Many of them are living with family members while waiting for their parents to arrive in heaven.

The Portal[10]

This is a place where those in heaven, both angels and the redeemed, can come to view activities on earth. It is similar to a huge balcony where spirit beings walk to the edge and look over onto a massive rotunda.

People are allowed to peer over the edge to see significant events in the lives of their family members, such as marriages, births, celebrations and especially the moment of salvation. As a result, those in heaven can still be a part of the lives of loved ones who are left on earth, sharing in their joy. In heaven there is no past, present or future; time exists in its full spectrum from creation to eternity.

At any given point in the portal hundreds are looking over the edge at the same time, but everyone sees something different: they all see their specific families on the earth. When someone observes a family member coming home to heaven, he races out to heaven's gate to greet him or her. They rejoice that the journey of life has been completed; the victory has been won.

> *"Since we are surrounded by so great a cloud of witnesses, let us lay aside every weight, and the sin which so easily ensnares us, and let us run with endurance the race that is set before us, looking unto Jesus the author and finisher of our faith" (Hebrews 12:1—2).*

Word University[11]

God's Word is of utmost importance to the building of faith on earth. If people have not had the opportunity to know and study the Bible, there will be a place where the Bible is taught in heaven. It's called Word University.

> *"Now I know in part, but then I shall know fully just as I also have been fully known." (I Corinthians 13:12b)*

Classes are held where the Scriptures are revealed by spiritual instructors or, at times, by the authors themselves. Imagine sitting under the tutelage of Moses, Samuel, David, Isaiah, John or Paul. The walls of the classrooms show scenes from the Bible; when viewed the scenes come alive, further illuminating the Word of God with startling reality.

Royal University[12]

Another purpose of education in heaven is to equip the saints to rule and reign with Christ when He returns to earth.

> *"And they lived and reigned with Christ for a thousand years" (Revelation 20:4c).*

When we arrive in heaven, we will have changed from our earthly bodies to our spirit beings. Only God knows the potential for these beings to be further trained and equipped for his work.

> *"Beloved, now we are children of God; and it has not yet been revealed what we shall be, but we know that when He is revealed, we shall be like Him, for we shall see Him as He is" (I John 3:2).*

Royal University is a place for that further training. It looks like a castle with woven tapestries in the hallways whose pictures come to life as one passes by. The archangel Michael, who commands the armies of heaven, is one of the trainers in the skills of leadership.

At the end of the course students are filled with wisdom, knowledge and love, ready to rule and reign with King Jesus. God's leaders in eternity will be filled with His glory and operate in total love, freedom and grace. They will be fully trained, supplied and equipped for eternal existence, according to God's plan.

The ruling and reigning will take place in the thousand-year period when Christ will reign on earth, during which there will be a continuing struggle between Satan and God's forces. At the end of this period Satan is defeated and sent to the bottomless pit.

> *"The devil, who deceived them, was cast into the lake of fire and brimstone…and…will be tormented day and night forever and ever" (Revelation 20:10).*

Hall of Knowledge[13]

The Hall of Knowledge is a type of library with vertical stacks that can be reached on a road of light moving through the air. The structure of the hall is made up of huge vertical columns that glow with the glory of God.

> *"That the God of our Lord Jesus Christ, the Father of glory, may give to you the spirit of wisdom and revelation in the knowledge of Him, the eyes of your understanding being enlightened; that you may know what is the hope of His calling, what are the riches of the glory of His inheritance in the saints…" (Ephesians 1:17—18)*

In this place of knowledge, a road of light moves up and down diamond-tipped columns to find a particular volume.

Once removed from its slot the book becomes a hologram; and the reader watches the book unfold, rather than reading it. There is information on every subject imaginable in heaven, except those things that are evil or unclean.

Memorials of Faith[14]

Although salvation comes only through faith in Jesus Christ, God expects that out of changed hearts, his children on earth will produce good works.

> *"But be doers of the word, and not hearers only, deceiving yourselves…he who looks into the perfect law of liberty and continues in it, and is not a forgetful hearer but a doer of the work, this one will be blessed in what he does." (James 1:22, 25)*

The writer of the book of James further emphasizes the importance of works as a proof of faith.

> *"Was not Abraham our father justified by works when he offered Isaac his son on the altar? Do you see that faith was working together with works, and by works faith was made perfect?" (James 2:22)*

God honors acts of obedience in response to faith, including works of kindness and generosity. Some visitors to heaven have seen memorials which celebrate these good deeds. These memorials take the form of parks with blooming flowers, cascading waterfalls and fountains. Sometimes the faces of the recipients of kindness are reflected in the water that flows through the memorials.

These memorials are oases of beauty to be enjoyed by all who dwell in heaven.

Special Gardens[15]

Many people have their own special gardens designed or tended for themselves or for a loved one not yet in heaven. For those who desire further intimacy with God, there are special gardens where one can meet Him. Our omniscient God who created the universe is also our personal Lord who wishes to spend time with His people so they may know the fullness of love He has in His heart for each one.

Hall of Nations[16]

Another place in heaven increases understanding among people from different nations. It is called the Hall of Nations and has numerous hallways projecting from a lobby area. Dozens of stations protrude from the walls of the hallways. As one approaches a station a platform rises from the floor. Standing on the platform, one prompts a floor-to-ceiling mirror-like object to appear. It is the color of burnished pewter and has reflective qualities. By pressing an arrow one can change his appearance to a different ethnicity with a costume typical of that group. Pressing another arrow returns the person to his original form.

A Caucasian can become Asian. An Indian can become African. Heaven is made up of people from all over the world, and in the Hall of Nations a visitor can experience what it is like to have a different heritage. In a loving God all His people are the same.

Creation Lab[17]

A very special location reveals mysteries of the ages and how evil entered the world. A place of both instruction and enlightenment, the Creation Lab allows people to witness the original creation of earth and the fall of Lucifer.

> *"I will remember Your wonders of old. I will also meditate on all Your work; and talk of Your deeds"* (Psalm 78:11—12 NASB).

Here the God of the universe provides His master plan for earth from the beginning of time. His creatures, especially mankind, play a significant role in the plan. In His infinite wisdom God laid out a perfect universe and anticipated intimate fellowship with His contented creation in a peaceable kingdom.

The Creation Lab story begins when a beautiful light fills a room in which a platform is holding a brilliant hologram. God appears and speaks to the void of space, and it begins to spin and form. God then pours water out of His hand to measure the ocean that surrounds a single land mass.

> *"In the beginning God created the heavens and the earth. The earth was without form and void; and darkness was on the face of the deep. And the Spirit of God was hovering over the face of the waters"* (Genesis 1:1—2).
>
> *"Then God said, 'Let there be light,' and there was light…God called the light Day, and the darkness He called Night"* (Genesis 1:3,5).

Next God creates an atmosphere in which He can sustain life, causing a huge vapor shield to surround the land mass with a continual heavy mist.

> *"Then God said, 'Let there be firmament in the midst of the waters, and let it divide the waters from the waters'" (Genesis 1:6).*

He speaks again, and vegetation forms: trees, plants and flowers. The aroma is intoxicating.

> *"Then God said, 'Let the earth bring forth grass, the herb that yields seed, and the fruit tree that yields fruit, according to its kind'" (Genesis 1:11).*

God then places creatures on the earth and in the water: dinosaurs, birds and fish. They are huge and varied beyond imagination. All the creatures live in harmony with one another. Evil has not yet entered creation.

> *"Then God said, 'Let the waters abound with an abundance of living creatures, and let birds fly above the earth across the face of the firmament of the heavens'" (Genesis 1:20).*

Millions of years pass, and violence interrupts the calm scene. War erupts in heaven; lightning thunders to earth with a loud clap. Archangel Michael has cast Lucifer, the most beautiful angel, out of heaven; and he has come streaking down to earth! A third of the angels whom Lucifer has deceived have come down with him.

"How you are fallen from heaven, O Lucifer, son of the morning! How you are cut down to the ground" (Isaiah 14:12).

Lucifer was created the most beautiful angel in all of creation. The prophet Ezekiel describes him.

"You were the seal of perfection, full of wisdom and perfect in beauty. You were in Eden, the garden of God. Every precious stone was your covering" (Ezekiel 28:12—13a).

In his pride Lucifer wanted to replace God as the one to be worshipped by all the other creatures in the universe.

"For you have said in your heart: I will ascend into heaven; I will exalt my throne above the stars of God. ...I will ascend above the heights of the clouds, I will be like the Most High" (Isaiah 14:13—14).

Lucifer is angry to be thrown down from heaven, and he takes up dominion on earth. In his fallen state Lucifer is the embodiment of evil and rebellion, and his hatred enters into the beauty of God's creation, causing a barren wilderness to emerge where once there was a verdant land.

God's creatures are no longer satisfied to eat His provision from grasses and fruits. They become fearful and suspicious, preying on one another for food. Controlled by Lucifer, also called Satan or the devil, God's wonderful earth is defiled and returns to a primitive state.

"I beheld the earth, and indeed it was without form, and void; and the heavens, they had no light. I beheld the

> *mountains, and indeed they trembled, and all the hills moved back and forth. I beheld, and indeed the fruitful land was a wilderness" (Jeremiah 4:23—24,26).*

When evil and destruction have had their fill, God acts; He reaches across space and breaks the water vapor shield. Billions of gallons of water hit the earth, separating the single land mass into pieces, forming the continents. Mountains rise, valleys fall; creatures are buried between the layers of the earth. The water persists until all the earth is covered. God leans forward and blows on the earth; ice forms, and darkness covers the earth. Millions of years pass.

Powerful streaks of light come from heaven, and the Spirit of God hovers over the frozen planet. God blows again, and the ice melts. God has determined to recreate the wonderful earth Satan has polluted. This time God will enter into His creation with a plan for salvation. All members of the Holy Trinity watch while God establishes the earth as we know it.

God speaks, and light is formed. The "days" of creation follow, measured according to eternity's timetable, not the twenty-four cycles of man. From God's hand come atmosphere, plants, animals and eventually man and woman.

> *"Then God saw everything that He had made, and indeed it was very good" (Genesis 1:31).*

The Creation Lab is the place where God shows His power as creator of the universe. It visually explains that God created the earth and everything on it; then He created people with whom He wanted a relationship. Those who have gone to heaven have accepted His offer of redemption and are joined with God for all eternity.

The rest of the story of God pursuing and revealing Himself to man is found in the Old Testament as it chronicles the tempestuous relationship between a loving God and rebellious mankind. In His infinite majesty God had a plan to rescue the earth from Lucifer's control and bring His beloved humans back to Himself.

Only in the New Testament do we have the fulfillment of God's plan in the life, death and resurrection of Jesus Christ, who was present with God the Father and the Holy Spirit at creation. God's Son was obedient, coming to earth, following God's path to the restoration of forever intimacy with His creatures. By receiving salvation through Jesus Christ, all humans can be restored to fellowship with the Father and can join Him in His amazing heaven.

Heavenly life is filled with the wonders of the universe, beings and places God had intended for His people from the beginning of time. It is a Garden of Eden, amplified to perfection where God and His people meet, laugh and play together. What's more, God has a delightful sense of humor. He understands our need to be playful and entertained. He has even provided pleasures far more imaginative and splendid than any flights of fancy can conceive. God's people can enjoy amazing entertainment possibilities forever in this place of heavenly bliss.

CHAPTER 6

HEAVENLY ENTERTAINMENT

Amusement Park[18]

GOD HAS CREATED ENDLESS opportunities to enjoy eternity. He is a God who rejoices when we are happy. In the midst of heaven is an amusement park with huge gates of ornate gold. The gates are not used for security because evil does not exist in heaven, but only to designate the park's location within the vast area of heaven. The amusement park is filled with rides that provide fun and thrills, but absolutely no danger. Because there is no chance of injury, rides can move with greater speed and give more excitement than those on earth. The rides are free, and people can enjoy them as often as they wish.

The Rush[19]

One of the favorite rides in the amusement park is a roller coaster called Rush. People laugh and scream as the cars race down the track. The cars have no wheels and are propelled on a cushion of light. Light comes from everywhere; it is in everything as a source of energy and fuel. Because there is no night, there are no shadows, and light is always present and fully available.

The amusement park also provides ways to win incredible rewards, eat delicious food and see fascinating shows. The park has nothing disgusting, grotesque or fearful anywhere, only imaginative, unusual and mind-blowing ways to have fun.

Fly By[20]

A second attraction in the amusement park is something called Fly By where people can learn to fly, not in airplanes and not because people have wings like angels. But in Peter-Pan fashion people are propelled through the air. Evidently it takes a while to gain proficiency in flying, but for the brave it is another fun activity a loving Father has created to give happiness to His children.

Reality Theater[21]

God, as the creator of all things, has given humankind the ability to develop many kinds of technology. In fact, God is continually giving people on earth new ideas to enhance life, but heaven is far more advanced than our lowly planet.

During the last century cinema has gone from silent films to sound production; from black and white to color; from two dimensional features to 3D. But in heaven people go a step further and actually perform in well-known films, becoming live actors in famous westerns or playing the role of heroes or heroines in romantic comedies.

Loved ones and family members can watch the performance and cheer on the one who has replaced the star on the screen. In fact, the screen itself opens up to a stage; and the film becomes a live, moving performance with real scenery backgrounds and plotline action.

Advertising for a film is live also. One passing through a lobby where future features are announced is drawn into a scene as if in a hologram with action all around. Patrons don't just view an upcoming movie; they can decide to join it by signing up to be part of the film as an actor.

Theaters themselves have more advanced designs. They have the latest in seating comfort for the audience, with uniquely shaped, wrap-around seats that conform to the shape of each sitter.

Only material that is edifying is kept in heaven for God's beloved children. Of course, there will be no movie or subject matter that contains immorality of any kind, including seductive or sexual content, nudity, graphic violence, profane or crude language. God is a holy God!

> *"But shall by no means enter it anything that defiles, or causes an abomination or a lie, but only those who are written in the Lamb's Book of Life" (Revelation 21:27).*

Surf Park-Wipeout[22]

At the base of a huge mountain in heaven is an enormous surf park called Wipeout. Waves generated by the water coming from the top of the mountain crash into a blue lagoon at the bottom, surging forward toward a beach. Surfers catch the waves coming out of the lagoon and ride them all the way to the sea.

Other types of water activity are in the park also. Whales and sea animals are able to interact with spirit beings, reestablishing the friendship between God's creatures not known since Adam and Eve in the Garden of Eden before the advent of sin.

Remember-When Gallery[23]

Another unusual form of entertainment is found in the Remember-When Gallery. If human life seems void of memorable moments, God's perfect memory will prove that life had precious times to savor. The life of each person in heaven has been recorded into mini movies that can be viewed with joy forever. The best of life on earth will be on these films, not hard times or tragedies or sinful experiences. Only happy moments that were significant or rewarding are preserved and can be viewed by spirit beings in their own private theaters.

Sports[24]

For sports enthusiasts heaven will not be disappointing. God has given people with athletic abilities a way to make use of them for eternity. But with evil absent danger will not prevent athletes from engaging in the most extreme sports.

A variety of games will be played: golf, football, basketball, fishing, water sports, horse racing. Every kind of friendly activity known on earth will be exercised in heaven. Who knows? God's people may even enjoy games not yet invented.

Heavenly life will be awesome with God's love at the center of all activities. From heavenly beings to heavenly places and heavenly entertainment, God has prepared a place beyond our fondest dreams. The wildest imagination cannot begin to fathom what God has created for laughter and enjoyment in heaven. All the wholesome pleasures of earth will be multiplied a hundred-fold. We know God is powerful in His goodness to us, but why has He created this incredible heaven?

CHAPTER 7

HEAVENLY LOVE: "SONG OF SONGS"

WHY DID GOD CREATE an amazing place to share with people at the end of their earthly existence? Why did He create the heavens and the earth at the beginning of time? How can we fathom the driving force of a God with the power to hold eternity in His hand?

God's reason for heaven is to dwell together with His beloved spirit beings in a world of happiness and joy that is free of Satan's power. In sending Jesus, God's Son, to suffer and die in our place, God proved His endless love for a humanity lost in sin. Heaven is further affirmation of that love.

How do we understand God's enormous love? In Scripture we repeatedly see a God who establishes a relationship with His people and speaks to them in acts of loving kindness. God's love to His people in Scripture reveals the kind of fellowship God desires to have with all people. For instance, the cries of the heart of David, shepherd and king, preserved in the psalms define a precious intimacy with God.

In the Bible we have an entire book devoted to a description of love, albeit human love. We have a picture in the Song of Songs of commitment and loyalty that unite human lovers in a bond that is only a foretaste of heavenly love. Yet from this picture we can glimpse the passion and devotion God has for His beloved creation.

Let's look at how the two lovers in the *Song of Songs* develop their love for each other. Their passion will provide clues to the love the Father has for His beloved people.

Chapter 1

The woman is the first to speak. She begins *Song of Songs* by sharing her openness to her lover's affection. *"Let him kiss me with the kisses of his mouth. For your love is better than wine, your anointing oils are fragrant."*

In a hot climate, where baths were infrequent, anointing oils changed unpleasant odors to wafting fragrances. She recognized him by these perfumes. She says, *"Draw me after you, let us make haste."* She admires him with the respect of a sovereign; perhaps he was King Solomon. But she says with delight, *"The king has brought me into his chamber."* She is eager to be with him.

"Tell me, you whom by soul loves, where you pasture your flock." She is asking where he spends his days; she wants to be near him.

Then the man speaks. *"O fairest among women, follow the tracks of the flock."* He acknowledges her unsurpassed beauty and tells her where she can find him. He is encouraging her to follow him.

He gazes upon her and sees her beauty. He describes her cheeks and her neck as attractive adornments, strings of jewels. He wants to give her ornaments of gold and silver to enhance her beauty.

> *"I compare you, my love,…your cheeks are comely with ornaments, your neck with strings of jewels. We will make you ornaments of gold, studded with silver."*

Now the woman paints a picture of her king on his couch with her so close that her perfume gives forth a lovely fragrance. He lies on her breasts and, like blossoms, prepares to offer her the fruit of his manliness.

> *"While the king was on his couch, my nard gave forth its fragrance. My beloved is to me a bag of myrrh that lies between my breasts. My beloved is to me a cluster of henna blossoms in the vineyards…"*

The king speaks again of her beauty and tenderness. *"Ah, you are beautiful, my love, ah, you are beautiful…truly lovely… As a lily among brambles so is my love among maidens."* Picture a delicate, vulnerable blossom placed in and contrasted to a rough, prickly shrub. There is a suggestion of his desire to protect her.

Chapter 2

The woman, in turn, compares her beloved to a fruitful apple tree that has been placed in the forest.

"As an apple tree among the trees of the wood, so is my beloved among young men. With great delight I sat in his shadow, and his fruit was sweet to my taste. He brought me to the banqueting house, and his intention toward me was love."

She longs for more of him, but at the same time she gives a warning. Love has a timing; it has to be determined by a mutual readiness and commitment. She says, *"I adjure you, O daughters of Jerusalem…do not stir up or awaken love until it is ready!"*

The next section of *Song of Songs* rhapsodizes about springtime, which is the normal time of fertility, when the earth awakens from sleep and flowers and animals prepare for their most glorious season of reproducing.

The woman is the one who beholds her beloved; she compares him to a light-hearted, graceful deer leaping over the hills to come to her, longing for her from outside her house.

> *"The voice of my beloved! Look, he comes, leaping upon the mountains, bounding over the hills. My beloved is like a gazelle or a young stag. Look, there he stands behind our wall, gazing in at the windows, looking through the lattice."*

He calls for her and bids her come to him. All of creation is taking delight in procreation; now is the time for lovers to partake of the blossoms of life that produce fruit. He says:

"Arise, my love, my fair one, and come away; for now the winter is past; the rain is over and gone. The flowers appear on the earth; the time of singing has come, and the voice of the turtledove is heard in our land. The fig tree puts forth its figs, and the vines are in blossom, they give forth fragrance. Arise, my love, my fair one; and come away, O my dove, to the clefts of the rock in the covert of the cliff, let me see your face, let me hear your voice, for your voice is sweet, and your face is lovely."

He suggests that together they can even subdue those little "foxes" that peck at and consume with irritation the fruit of love before it fully matures. They can chase away the spoilers of the harvest, the spoilers of their love. He says, *"Catch us the foxes, the little foxes, that ruin the vineyards—for our vineyards are in blossom."* Now is the time.

She responds, *"My beloved is mine, and I am his."* They have committed to each other in a binding love that merely awaits its fulfillment.

Chapter 3

The next section is like a dream. The woman seeks her beloved upon her bed at night. She seems to search for him through the streets and asks those she sees if they have seen her king. *"Have you seen him whom my soul loves?"* she asks.

But she continues, *"Scarcely had I passed them, when I found him whom my soul loves. I held him, and would not let him go until I brought him into my mother's house, and into the chamber of her that conceived me."* The bed is ready for them; she has learned about the ways of love from her mother.

But again the woman gives warning. Prepared as she seems for consummation and eager as she is for love, she pauses. *"Do not stir up or awaken love until it is ready!"* This is the second time she cautions not to force love but let feelings evolve and love develop as it will. Love must wait for the proper time. Total sexual consummation is yet to come.

Now the bridegroom is ready; he comes in the custom of his day with his mighty men around him, armed to protect their leader. They are bearing him on a throne of purple, gold and silver. He is crowned with glory on the day of his wedding. He is filled with gladness of heart.

> *"What is coming up from the wilderness like a column of smoke, perfumed with myrrh and frankincense, with all the fragrant powders of the merchant? Look, it is… Solomon! Around [him] are sixty mighty men…all equipped with swords, and expert in war…because of alarms by night.*
>
> *"Look, O daughters of Zion, at King Solomon, at the crown with which his mother crowned him on the day of his wedding, on the day of gladness of heart."*

Chapter 4

The bride, too, is ready. She is beautiful, and her king extols the vision of her. He compares her eyes, hair, teeth, lip, mouth, neck and breasts to the beauty of commonly understood examples of the culture of the day. His loved one epitomizes those things that give him pleasure and satisfaction.

> *"How beautiful you are, my love, how very beautiful! Your eyes are doves…Your hair is like a flock of goats*

moving down the slopes of Gilead. Your teeth are like a flock of shorn ewes that have come up from washing. Your lips are like a crimson thread, and your mouth is lovely. Your cheeks are like halves of pomegranates. Your neck is like the tower of David. Your two breasts are like two fawns…that feed among the lilies."

He proclaims, *"You are altogether beautiful, my love, there is no flaw in you. Come with me…, my bride, come with me. …You have ravished my heart, my sister, my bride, you have ravished my heart with a glance of your eyes, with one jewel of your necklace. How sweet is your love, my sister, my bride!"*

He has begun to experience her. He smells her body; he kisses her lips; he breathes in her perfumes. *"How much better is your love than wine, and the fragrance of your oils than any spice! Your lips distill my nectar, my bride, honey and milk are under your tongue; the scent of your garments is like the scent of Lebanon."*

But her inner spaces are still closed to him. The choicest fruits of the harvest are still unavailable until she invites him into those secret places of her heart and body.

He describes her as *"a garden locked, a fountain sealed…a garden fountain, a well of living water, and flowing streams…,"* until the bride opens wide to his love and says, *"Awake, O north wind, and come, O south wind! Blow upon my garden that its fragrance may be wafted abroad. Let my beloved come to his garden, and eat its choicest fruits."*

The time is right; the marriage can be consummated. With great excitement the groom says, *"I come to my garden; I gather my myrrh with my spice. I eat my honeycomb with my honey. I drink my wine with my milk."* He partakes of the joy of completion in the consummation of love with his bride.

Then the bridegroom rejoices with his friends and bids them, *"Eat, friends, drink, and be drunk with love."*

Chapter 5

But another dream-like sequence presents a different scenario: The woman is asleep, and she hears her beloved knocking on the door. He is ready for love; he must have her right away, but she is not ready. She has prepared for sleep, not for love.

She rises, gathers her clothing, makes herself ready and opens for him, but he is gone. He did not wait for her. He did not wait for his supremely beautiful loved one. He went elsewhere with his yearning. She says, *"I opened to my beloved, but my beloved had turned and was gone."*

She is left alone, longing for him. She goes out to search for her beloved, but this time she cannot find him; and she is abused while searching. Other men encounter her on the streets; they take away her clothes and mistreat her.

"They beat me, they wounded me, they took away my mantle." She is left with unfulfilled and violated love, and she experiences instead the defilement of those who care nothing about her. They only wanted her readiness for love, her vulnerability.

She asks her friends to find him for her. *"I adjure you, O daughters of Jerusalem, if you find my beloved, tell him this, I am faint with love."* But her friends mock her. *"What is your beloved more than another beloved?"* Why does she seek him more than someone else? they ask.

She describes him as *"radiant and ruddy, distinguished among ten thousand."* This time it is her turn to describe his features—his head, eyes, cheeks, lips, arms, legs, body—using the environment of the culture to compare him to beauty in life around them.

> *"His head is the finest gold; his locks are wavy, black as a raven. His eyes are like doves beside springs of water, bathed in milk, fitly set. His cheeks are like beds of spices, yielding fragrance. His lips are lilies, distilling liquid myrrh. His arms are rounded gold, set with jewels. His body is ivory work, encrusted with sapphires. His legs are alabaster columns set upon bases of gold."*

She concludes by saying, *"His appearance is like Lebanon, choice as the cedars. His speech is most sweet, and he is altogether desirable. This is my beloved and this is my friend, O daughters of Jerusalem."* She does not want another lover; she wants him whom her heart loves.

Chapter 6

"Where has your beloved gone, O fairest among women?" her friends ask. *"Which way has your beloved turned, that we may seek him with you?"* She answers, *"My beloved has gone down to his garden,"* but she reminds herself of their commitment. *"I am my beloved's, and my beloved is mine; he pastures his flock among the lilies."*

Her beloved had left her to pursue the rest of his gardens, and before he knew it he had satisfied his burning desire and, in the process, forsaken the woman he loved. In haste he had forgotten his perfect one and her position of extreme value to him, above all others.

He explains, *"I went down to the nut orchard, to look at the blossoms of the valley, to see whether the vines had budded, whether the pomegranates were in bloom. Before I was aware, my fancy set me in a chariot…"*

But now he recognizes that she is set apart for her grace and beauty. He calls her back to himself. *"Return, return, that we may look upon you."* He reassures her of his love as he again describes her matchless beauty. His commitment is renewed and deepened beyond the immediacy of passion.

Chapter 7

He sees her in a new light; he calls her a queenly maiden. He describes her body from her feet to her head with expressions of praise. He says, *"How fair and pleasant you are, O loved one, delectable maiden!…The scent of your breath [is] like apples, and your kisses like the best wine that goes down smoothly, gliding over lips and teeth."*

She is reassured, and she wants to be with him forever to accompany him always, so she can love him wherever he is. *"I am my beloved's and his desire is for me. Come, my beloved, let us go forth into the fields, and lodge in the villages; let us go out early to the vineyards, and see whether the vines have budded, whether the grape blossoms have opened and the pomegranates are in bloom. There I will give you my love."*

Chapter 8

Her desire has been quickened; she seeks after love and longs for the embrace of her beloved. She explains her passion to him. *"I would lead you and bring you into the house of my mother, and into the chamber of the one who bore me. I would give you spiced wine to drink, the juice of my pomegranates."*

She further fantasizes, *"O that his left hand were under my head, and that his right hand embraced me!"* But again she gives warning. *"Do not stir up or awaken love until it is ready."* Love is a powerful, magnificent emotion, and becoming aroused can cause fury if it is not in the right time and place.

She declares that her commitment is enduring with strong emotion. Passion is as powerful as death. She is bound to him in love. She says, *"Set me as a seal upon your heart, as a seal upon your arm; for love is strong as death, passion fierce as the grave. Its flashes are flashes of fire, a raging fire. Many waters cannot quench love, neither can floods drown it. If one offered for love all the wealth of his house, it would be utterly scorned."* True love is valued above all other possessions.

She acknowledges her faithfulness to him alone. *"My vineyard, my very own, is for myself."* But she looks to those who come after her, who are young and have not yet known love. When they are in the time of prime harvest they need to lift up their voices and declare their readiness. *"O you who dwell in the gardens, my companions are listening for your voice; let me hear it."*

Future generations, too, will experience love; and after the tempest of emotion is passed, enduring love will bring peace and fruitfulness. All who dwell in that fruitfulness of life, who await and long for re-creation, who listen for the voice of the beloved, will still hear it calling to them in the garden of love.

Do you have a picture of the breathless delights of love and passion? Do you see the beauty of nature and the habits of the culture in which this love unfolds? Do you sense the all-encompassing desire the lovers have for each other? Do you see the continuity of love from one generation to another as young lovers prepare to follow the pattern of their forebears into life-producing love? Do you understand the yearning of God for His people mirrored in human love?

What is the first thing one hears from a lover or bridegroom about his beloved, his bride? She is beautiful! He sees her face, her form, her movements, her mysterious ways. What does the bride see in her loved one? He is handsome, strong, witty and desirable.

In the *Song of Songs*, the bridegroom proclaims the beauty of the bride, gives her gifts to enhance it, and showers her with goodness. She, in turn, wants to be with him, adoring him, receiving his protection. She gives of herself in gratitude for his love.

This picture of love set in an earthly time and place illustrates the love God has for us. He wants to dwell with us continually to give us joy now and for eternity and to receive our love and adoration forever. He is creator and king of the universe, a position of power and might. But through Jesus He is also the lover of our souls, the holy bridegroom; and we are His spotless bride. Our response to His love now on earth and in heaven forever is worship and praise! The beloved dances around the throne of God expressing love and joy. She whispers the name of Jesus in supplication and worship.

We have seen the beauty of heaven, a glorious place in which God dwells with His beloved people. Above the clouds are found a delightful heavenly life, beings that serve and love God, stimulating places to go to learn and grow, exciting activities for play and laughter. We understand the model of perfect love as developed between humans and exemplified in the bridegroom Jesus Christ.

How now can we show our gratitude to God for all He has given us on earth and in heaven? What does He ask of us in return for His abundant blessings? What was the coveted gift of devotion that Satan tried to wrestle from God, causing Satan's expulsion from heaven?

The answer is found in praise and worship. God delights in our adoration and love. Our gatherings to honor God on earth usually include some kind of worship. We can show our love through expressions of dance, song, visual art, intimacy in prayer and creative meditation where we receive ideas and inspiration from the throne of God. And in heaven, as on earth, worship often is associated with music.

CHAPTER 8

HEAVENLY WORSHIP

IT IS IMPOSSIBLE TO go anywhere in heaven without music literally "appearing." It is more than sound; music actually has colors, sometimes in the shape of ribbons with words streaming by. Music has a tangible presence. Music is part of worship, which happens continuously in heaven. Angelic beings and the redeemed join together in beautiful songs that float above the people on the way to the throne room where music creates a sweet aroma before the Father.

The throne room is the place where God dwells and receives the praises of His people. Dancing folks and heavenly beings declare their love for the Father, creating a scene of reverence and awe. The glory of the Lord is so powerful that at times worshippers fall prostrate before the throne.

The throne room of God the Father is available to all who dwell in heaven. The Father welcomes anyone who wishes to see Him or the rest of the Holy Trinity. In fact, the Father, Son and Holy Spirit are one being, going in and out of each other. They think alike, feel alike and love alike, and are all equally holy. Worship on earth or in heaven honors all three members. Praying to one is talking to all of them. Prayer and worship create intimacy with the Godhead. The purpose of life on earth is to become part of the divine family of faith, headed by the Father, Son and Holy Spirit, and praise them forever.

> *"We who first hoped in Christ have been destined and appointed to live for the praise of his glory" (Ephesians 1:12 RSV).*

Worship and prayers on earth are collected and presented to the Father as incense. Sweet fragrances continually fill the throne room as God's people love Him with song, instruments and dance.

> *"From the rising of the sun, even to its going down, My name shall be great among the Gentiles; in every place incense shall be offered to My name" (Malachi 1:11).*

Sometimes prayers are received in heaven as a bolt of light. When they rise to the Father they gather together and explode into one bright penetrating beam. They linger in the throne room as a powerful aroma of incense delighting the senses.

> *"Let my prayer be set before You as incense, the lifting up on my hands as the evening sacrifice" (Psalm 141:2).*

God relishes different ways of praising Him. Dancers create a spiritual tapestry woven beneath their moving feet, twirling around the Father's throne room. The tapestry is then placed in a praise gallery to be viewed by those in heaven. God collects precious evidence of adoration and praise for all to enjoy in His heavenly kingdom.

Likewise, ribbons of beautiful color stream from the mouths of those who praise in the spirit realm. These, too, weave a tapestry that becomes a masterpiece, proclaiming love to God. The same thing happens when instruments are played for His glory. Imagine the visual beauty created by these expressions of praise!

With each stroke of the brush artists who praise God in their work release musical notes that assemble into a beautiful symphony dedicated to the Father. When the artist sees the masterpiece in heaven, actual melodies will come forth from the painting.

Praise releases love for God, but it also releases power. God lives and acts in praises, effectively defeating evil on earth and accumulating treasures for eternity in heaven.

"The Lord inhabits the praises of His people" (Psalm 22:3, KJV).

Praises swirl around heaven for eternity as a reminder of God's love and the victory of good over evil. God is delighted with the praise and adoration of His people. It is an act of submission to His holy presence. It is a gift of repayment to God for His goodness and mercy in redeeming us from our sins. Praise also gladdens the hearts of believers on earth as in heaven, bringing them inexpressible joy. Praise lifts us into the throne room of the Father even while we remain on earth. It provides power and victory over the devil and gives us a glimpse of eternity.

CHAPTER 9

HELL:
DON'T GO THERE!

Another journey might await us at the end of our earthly lives. It's the alternative to heaven, and it is the place where Satan dwells along with the angels that fell with him from heaven early in time. It is hell, and we could go there too.

We all sin; sin has consequences. It separates us from a Father too holy to look upon our sin. Isaiah 59 tells us God's reaction to sin. He grieves that Satan in his anger toward God snatches God's precious children on earth away from His heavenly kingdom by subtle fear, intimidation and temptation. Isaiah says,

> *"Your iniquities have separated you from your God; and your sins have hidden His face from you, so that He will not hear…We look for light, but there is darkness!*

> *For brightness, but we walk in blackness!...We stumble at noonday as at twilight. We are dead men in desolate places...We look for justice, but there is none; for salvation, but it is far from us. For our transgressions are multiplied before [God], and our sins testify against us; for our transgressions are with us, and as for our iniquities, we know them" (Isaiah 59, selected verses).*

That sin which is pervasive in all our lives gives us a completely different end-of-life experience.[25] Upon death one begins to feel a sinister presence, causing flesh to tremble. Demons appear and take hold of the person with claw-like hands, tugging and pulling him downward until everything disappears into darkness. The new arrival to hell is held in chains of bondage and encircled by demons in a dank, scary place.

One author describes the hell he visited with creatures all around: "These creatures were not of this natural world...they were entirely evil, and they were gazing at me with pure, unrestrained hatred."[26]

The rotten stench of death fills the place. Tormenting sounds of screaming and moaning come from agonized souls already plunged into vast, pitch black nothingness. Darkness and evil have control over the person. Satan now owns the damned soul.

Entering the yawning mouth of the underworld, the condemned person feels pain, agony and fear. Every kind of torture awaits him as demons yell in glee and begin to mutilate the unsuspecting victim. Fire and smoke are everywhere, causing all the inhabitants to languish in searing heat, surrounded by every imaginable horror. There is no food or drink, only continual starvation, dehydration and loneliness. All hope is gone!

In hell there is no contact with other human beings. From the screaming and cursing of people and demons, noisy irritation swirls in the heads of every suffering person. People resent each other and wallow in self-pity. There is no rest, no peace, just utter exhaustion and terror; and there is no escape…ever!"

The psalmist describes this place known by God.

> *"You have laid me in the lowest pit, in darkness, in the depths. Your wrath lies heavy upon me, and you have afflicted me with all your waves. You have put away my acquaintances far from me; You have made me an abomination…I am shut up and cannot get out"* *(Psalm 88:6—8).*

God created this place of torment, not for humankind, but for the devil and his angels. God's intention was never that His beloved mankind should end up in hell. To the contrary, when God saw that this horrible pit had become the destination for wretched, sinful mankind, He knew He needed to act.

He had pity on those who in ignorance believed the lies of Satan and failed to choose eternity with God the Father. Isaiah 59 continues with what God did about our sinful condition which we inherited from Adam way back in the beginning of time.

> *"Then the Lord saw it, and it displeased Him that there was no justice. He saw that there was no man, and wondered that there was no intercessor; therefore His own arm brought salvation for Him; and His own righteousness, it sustained Him"* *(Isaiah 59, selected verses).*

God Himself took action to free mankind from the jaws of hell, the underworld of darkness.

> *"He put on righteousness as a breastplate, and a helmet of salvation on His head; he put on the garments of vengeance for clothing, and was clad with zeal as a cloak…The Redeemer will come…to those who turn from transgression…" (Isaiah 59:17,20).*

God sent His Son to bring us salvation and rescue us from sin, death and hell. In Isaiah 60, the description of the victory of light coming into the world continues:

> *"Arise, shine; for your light has come! And the glory of the Lord is risen upon you. For behold, the darkness shall cover the earth, and deep darkness the people; but the Lord will arise over you, and His glory will be seen upon you…Then you shall see and become radiant, and your heart shall swell with joy…And I will glorify the house of My glory…For in My wrath I struck you, but in My favor I have had mercy on you…You shall know that I, the Lord am your Savior" (Isaiah 60, selected verses).*

When we have violated the laws of the king of the universe, we feel remorse. We recognize that we have fallen short of the best God has for us, and we are sorry. Early in time God saw our need and armed Himself for battle. He came down to earth in the person of His Son to fight for our deliverance. He died and accomplished the victory through His resurrection from the dead, defeating Satan, the ultimate enemy.

Now, given our natural, unredeemed state, how do we come to a holy God and receive His forgiveness? The answer is found in Jesus Christ, the redeemer God sent to pluck us back from hell's pit and give us the amazing heaven God intended for us from before creation.

God has already chosen us for heaven, but by the default of original sin we are bound for hell, unless we choose His redeemer. God has given us free will to make a choice. Our job is to accept God's offer of eternity where we live with Him in the wonderful place filled with joy forever. The prophet Jeremiah gives the pathway: seeking God and His forgiveness with our whole heart.

> *"You will seek Me and find Me when you search for Me with all your heart" (Jeremiah 29:13).*

God knows the heart of each person, and He longs for true repentance that will reunite each of us with Him in His kingdom. If you are uncertain of whether your destination at the moment of death will be heaven or hell, please talk to God now. Sincerely confess your sins, receive His salvation and know that you will be joined with loved ones and friends in heaven forever.

> *"If you confess with your mouth Jesus as Lord and believe in your heart that God raised Him from the dead, you will be saved" (Romans 10:9 NASB)*
>
> *"He who believes and is baptized will be saved" (Mark 16:16).*

Use these words as you have a conversation with the God who loves you more than you can imagine:

> "Lord God, I acknowledge You as the one who has created me. You have loved me with an everlasting

love. I confess that I have sinned and am in need of Your forgiveness. From the deepest places of my heart I ask You to forgive my sins and cleanse me from all unrighteousness through the blood of Jesus, Your Son. I believe He died for me. Thank You for Your grace and mercy. Receive me into Your kingdom. I ask this in the mighty name of Jesus Christ. Amen."

If you have made this honest confession now, as a new creation you can declare the words of the apostle Paul in his letter to the Galatians.

> *"I have been crucified with Christ and I no longer live, but Christ lives in me. The life I live in the body, I live by faith in the Son of God, who loved me and gave himself for me" (Galatians 2:20, NIV).*

God will continue to guide you by the Holy Spirit into the new life He has for you on earth. A good start is to read the Bible. It is a guide for life as the Holy Spirit teaches you from the inside out. The gospel of John in the New Testament is a valuable introduction to Jesus' teachings.

> *"Your word is a lamp to my feet and a light to my path"* (Psalm 119:105).

Another way to righteous living is to practice keeping God's commandments, summarized in the Ten Commandments found in Exodus, chapter 20 or Deuteronomy, chapter 5. The fellowship of other believers also promotes spiritual growth and provides encouragement in faith.

> *"Blessed are those who do His commandments that they may have the right to the tree of life, and may enter through the gates into the city" (Revelation 22:14).*

Death will come to each of us at our appointed time. As forgiven people we will be ready for it, and as God has forgiven us, so we can grant that same forgiveness to those we love. Anytime in life, but especially at the end of life, we can remember to say to our dear ones, "All is forgiven." Go in peace!

We are prepared to enter God's eternal kingdom, to join the saints who live in His light, who praise Him for his mercy and goodness.

> *"...giving thanks to the Father who has qualified us to be partakers of the inheritance of the saints in the light. He has delivered us from the power of darkness and conveyed us into the kingdom of the Son of His love, in whom we have redemption through His blood, the forgiveness of sins" (Colossians 1:12—14).*

God has provided a heaven that is beyond our comprehension. It means an existence of peace, joy and love shared with beings that are created to praise God forever. It means opportunities to be enriched with experiences of untold happiness. It means the ability to absorb God's love and worship Him forever. This is God's will for us. Accept His grace, be transformed by His love. Dwell in His courts of favor for all eternity. Heaven is amazing! It is God's desired destination for each person on earth.

> *"Amen. Even so, come, Lord Jesus! The grace of our Lord Jesus Christ be with you all. Amen" (Revelation 22:20—21).*

ENDNOTES

1. Kat Kerr, *Revealing Heaven* (Maitland, FL: Xulon Press, 2007), 33, 36. Kat Kerr, *Revealing Heaven II* (Maitland, FL: Xulon Press, 2010), 38.

2. Kerr, *Heaven II*, 42.

3. Kerr, *Heaven,* 82; *Heaven II*, 42.

4. Kerr, *Heaven,* 28; *Heaven II*, 36.

5. *davidwilkersontoday.blogspot.com/2012/09/jacobs-ladder.html*

6. Kerr, *Heaven,* 42; *Heaven II*, 118-121.

7. Kerr, *Heaven II*, 81-82.

8. Kerr, *Heaven,* 74.

9. Author Kerr describes nurseries in her two books: *Heaven,* 73-74; *Heaven II*, 76-77.

10. Portals are also described in Kerr, *Heaven,* 69-71; *Heaven II*, 109-110.

11. Word University is part of Kerr's visions in her second book, 46-47.

12. Kerr, *Heaven II*, 49.

13. Books become alive, as author Kerr describes: *Heaven II*, 56.

14. Good deeds are remembered. Kerr, *Heaven*, 97-98.

15. Kerr, *Heaven*, 27.

16. Kerr, *Heaven*, 91-94.

17. Kerr records the creation of the universe in her second book, 50-55.

18. Kerr, *Heaven*, 48.

19. Kerr, *Heaven*, 81.

20. Kerr, *Heaven*, 84.

21. Kerr, *Heaven*, 85-87.

22. Kerr, *Heaven II*, 104.

23. Kerr, *Heaven II*, 105.

24. Kerr, *Heaven II*, 123-124.

25. Kerr, *Heaven*, 38-39.

26. Bill Wiese, *23 Minutes in Hell* (Lake Mary, FL: Charisma House, 2006), 3

BIBLIOGRAPHY

Alcorn, Randy. *Heaven*. Carol Stream, IL: Tyndale House, 2004.

Bennett, Rita. *To Heaven and Back*. Grand Rapids, MI: Zondervan, 1976.

Burpo, Todd, with Lynn Vincent. *Heaven Is for Real*. Nashville, TN: Thomas Nelson, 2010.

Kerr, Kat. *Revealing Heaven*. Maitland, FL: Xulon Press, 2007.

Kerr, Kat. *Revealing Heaven II*. Maitland, FL: Xulon Press, 2010.

Piper, Don, with Cecil Murphey. *90 Minutes in Heaven*, Grand Rapids MI: Fleming Revell Publishing, 2004.

Thomas, Choo. *Heaven Is So Real!* Lake Mary, FL: Charisma House, 2003.

Wiese, Bill. *23 Minutes in Hell*. Lake Mary, FL: Charisma House, 2006.

ABOUT THE AUTHOR

THE YOUNGEST OF THREE daughters born to a Midwest pastor and his wife, Carolyn Turnquist Linn entered this world just as World War II began. She grew up in the church, warmed by the love and example of her father, a faithful minister of God's Word.

She met her husband in a church-related college. They married and moved to the West Coast after graduation. While living in the Midwest again briefly, the couple had two beautiful children born twelve months apart.

Carolyn began her career as an educator in California, teaching English and French on the secondary level. While the family was growing, she took her skills to the banking industry, writing educational materials. She retired from the community college foundation where she assisted in raising money for student scholarships.

The mental illness of Carolyn's husband, which developed early in their marriage, impacted the entire family. Yet it caused a reliance on a loving God who never disappointed them. Repeatedly the Lord sustained the household during the challenges of more than thirty years living with schizophrenia. The family continually witnessed a steadfast God in the midst of chaos and unpredictability.

In retirement the author, a cancer survivor, does volunteer work in addition to writing. From her experience with mental illness she encourages family members living with this difficult malady. She also ministers in her church and a local hospital where she frequently encounters people who are soon to complete their journeys on earth and enter into eternity, in either heaven or hell. She prays she will see them in God's amazing heaven.

Carolyn lives in Fresno, California. Her children and their exceptional families, including four grandchildren, live in Texas.